To my daughter Capucine

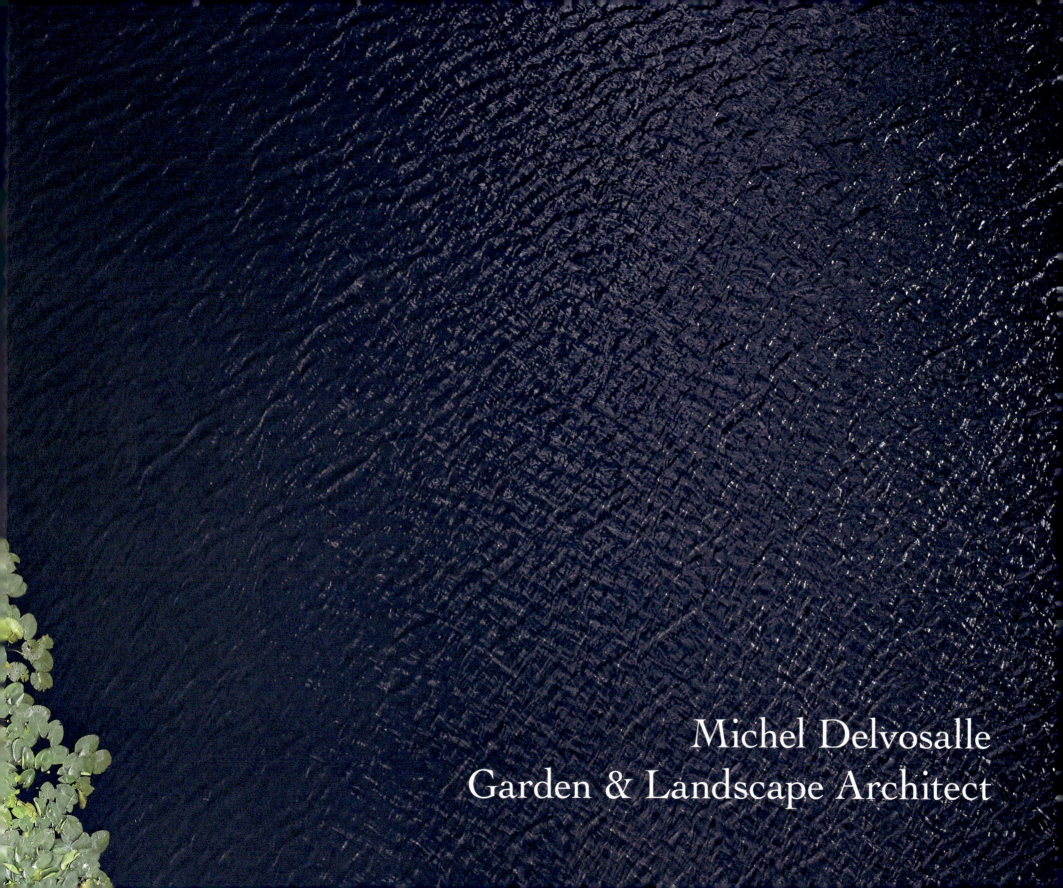
Michel Delvosalle
Garden & Landscape Architect

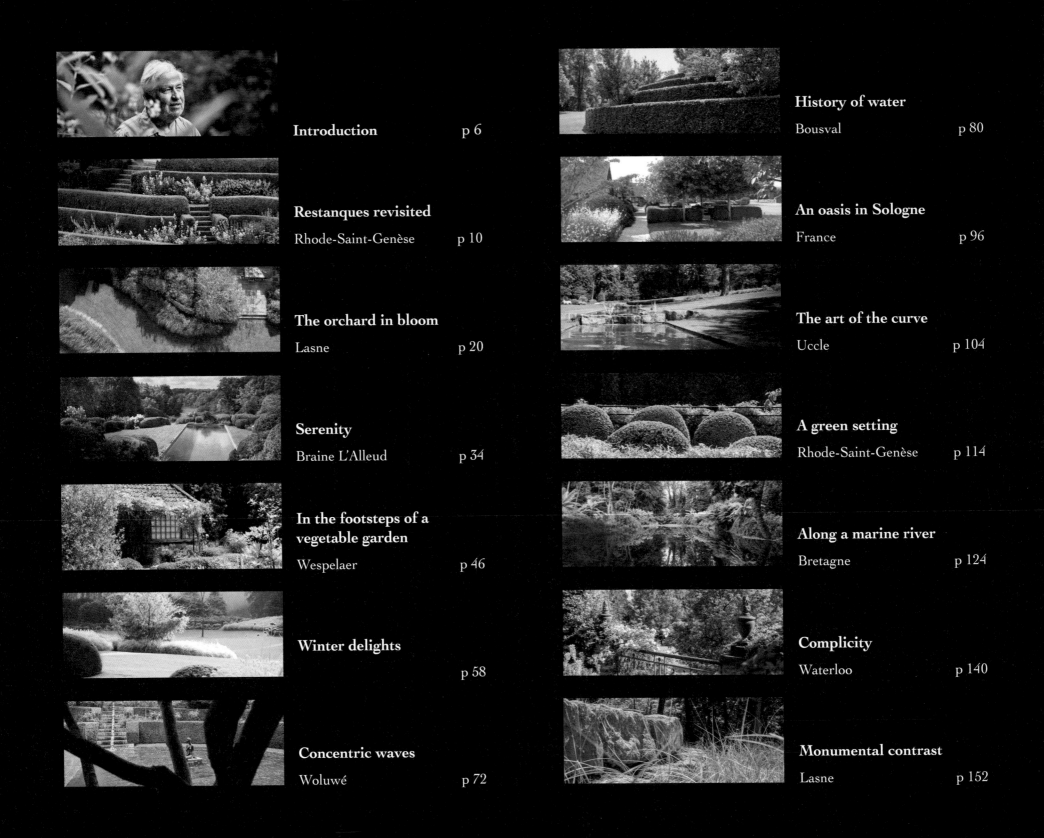

Introduction	p 6
Restanques revisited Rhode-Saint-Genèse	p 10
The orchard in bloom Lasne	p 20
Serenity Braine L'Alleud	p 34
In the footsteps of a vegetable garden Wespelaer	p 46
Winter delights	p 58
Concentric waves Woluwé	p 72
History of water Bousval	p 80
An oasis in Sologne France	p 96
The art of the curve Uccle	p 104
A green setting Rhode-Saint-Genèse	p 114
Along a marine river Bretagne	p 124
Complicity Waterloo	p 140
Monumental contrast Lasne	p 152

Return to the imagination of childhood
Tourneppe   p 160

Infinitudes
Ixelles   p 172

A landscape utopia
France   p 180

Ephemeral reflections
Ixelles   p 196

Harmony
Rhode-Saint-Genèse   p 206

Infinity of plants
Woluwé   p 218

Water games in the Ardennes
p 228

The joy of living

The moat

Provençal dreaml
France

The art of living at Mol
Ixelles

Golf des 7 fontaines
Braine L'Alleud

The flight
Rhode-Saint-Genèse

Brussels, City of Water

The idea of a publication was latent. Was a parenthesis in my creative life necessary?

I am bored with reading texts in books about gardens. I wanted a different form, one that would reflect our technological evolution. I therefore turned to a multitude of photographs accompanied by videos, which can be accessed using a "Quick Response" code. It allows you to step out of the image, to go through the text in visual or auditory animation... maybe olfactory one day...

This writing work has allowed me to research, to return to the places, and to reconnect with these beautiful people who have given me their trust. Although it was difficult to make a selection, the warm welcome I received gave me a real sense of satisfaction.

To rediscover the joy of creation, of graphic design next to the human relationship, so important, the reunion after these daily adventures, the confidence established, my passage to the next stage of my life. How pleasant it was!

I am probably endowed with a heightened sensitivity, which is open to the impregnation of the living space, I try to insert the human into nature.

I need to get a feel for the place, then comes a time of introspection, of getting out of the realm of reality to access the utopian realm, in the joy of interactive creation. Then a common thread, made of a multitude of small sketches in plan, perspective, volume, of shadow and colour merge into a logical plan.

The return to reality takes place during the collaboration in the office with my friend Pierre, my accomplice. The combination of our personalities gives rise to a balanced creation, a Delvosallian vision of space.

During the implementation of the plans, it is essential for me to set my feet in the ground, in the mud, so as to be able to change important details at any time, thanks in particular to the pragmatism and the assertions of all the contractors.

All these elements combined create a soothing balance: after these wounds inflicted on nature, the landscape heals.

To modify space, to remodel it, to give birth to a universe where one feels good, quite simply, is for me to touch the plenitude.

Michel Delvosalle
Landscape Architect

Biography

Passionate about nature and the harmony of landscapes,
Michel Delvosalle completed his studies as a landscape architect in 1972.
He immediately created his first office
for the development of public and private spaces.

His extremely varied career as a visionary garden artist,
creator of spaces and atmospheres, painter, sculptor and
landscape architect is far from ordinary.

If all the gardens of Michel Delvosalle have a strength and a particularism
that make them unique, there is one hallmark: the search for harmony
and the flexibility to adapt to places and people.

A selection of gardens created between 1982 - 2020.

The creator of these gardens is sensitive to the environment, people and nature. He translates dreams, interprets desires, accepts challenges, he combines the imaginary with the possible. He feels the nature of the land, tames it. He frees the imprisoned air, light and water.

Michel knows the texture of plants and weaves surprisingly natural combinations. Boxwood and laurel combine the delicacy of anemones and verbena. Michel loves contrasts. He draws curves that paint the landscape with rhododendrons, sage, lavender and roses. A palette of colours that changes with the seasons. He finds the sleeping Miró in trunks and stones and uncovers a garden of Van Gogh or Turner, hidden in a humble abandoned vegetable garden or a landscape by Gauguin buried on the edge of an almost dry stream.
He watches over them, breathing life into them, making them exist, for our happiness, in all their splendour.

Where once there was a desert, now ash trees and maple trees marvel us. A dance of branches. A sling of perovskia. A flutter of rushes. A tickle of grasses. Where there was a field of snowy stems, enclosed by steps teeming with ferns and white sedum. The shade of the plane trees, the firmness of the yew, the thickness of the ferns. And everywhere, a hum of light. Where there was once a puddle, he creates a pool, a pond, a waterfall, a water song.

Michel knows that each garden is a utopia that reminds us of the Garden of Eden. His gardens are criss-crossed by winding paths that allow you to enjoy the whole estate. This is why he creates places where human life is more beautiful, more gentle, more harmonious, more poetic. Closer to the memory of the Paradise that we have lost.

The gardens in this book are part of his work. They are witness to his immense talent, made up of a profound technical knowledge, a boundless creativity and a committed respect for nature. These gardens are the imprint not only of an excellent architect and landscape designer, but above all of a real artist. An artist who has never forgotten the child he was, the child who built the worlds he invented with sticks and wood. An artist who every day looks at the world with new eyes.

Enter his gardens.
Admire them.
Marvel.
Dream.

Matilde Martínez Sallés

Restanques revisited
Rhode-Saint-Genèse

"Michel created a splendid garden for us a few years ago from which we derive a great deal of satisfaction. He was right in many respects. The pronounced reliefs, the unusual pond, and the old stones that adorn the imposing terraces give a grandiose touch to the whole environment.
Moreover, this garden becomes more beautiful with time and we are encouraged to walk through it almost daily."

With the collaboration of Gregory le Grelle.

The general questioning of the property has been carried out in concert with the architects. The embankment has been adapted to the new accesses by the establishment of a subtle range of concealed earth retentions, box hedges, completed by steps, narrow walkways and pleasant rest areas. At different levels, we are free to perceive the whole harmoniously flowered.

The orchard in bloom
Lasne

"Thank you Michel
I love my garden
It is full of sweetness, of poetry
Last night there were lots of bees from my hives
Amongst the flowers
I love it…"

In the hilly landscape, a slightly sloping, boring lawn,
has been reshaped into flat areas along the edge of the slope,
planted with grasses and flowers.
By the play of undulating hedges in harmony with
the distant view, one loses oneself in a labyrinth of grassy paths,
one crosses a long gallery of flowers, planted with alternating wisteria,
clematis, and climbing roses.
A profusion of flowers surround the terraces: gaura, hesperis, perovskia,
in an orchard-like atmosphere.

Serenity
Braine-L'Alleud

"When the garden is only the humble reflection
of a perfect landscape, an extension...
When after 40 years, every day the emotion in front
of this beauty overwhelms you like a child meeting for
the first time the perfection of a flower picked by a bee...
the sweetness of living in a house nestled in the vegetation,
you slowly learn to meet the eternal!"

In addition to the construction of a passive solar house in 1982 on the south, a lush oasis of greenery surrounds the terraces, staircases and vegetable garden, leaving meadows for the horses.
The natural swimming pool blends with the distant pond below, bringing the water closer ... reflecting the sky.

In the footsteps of a vegetable garden
Wespelaer

"An old vegetable garden transformed into a buried garden, enough to enchant the hosts of this place."

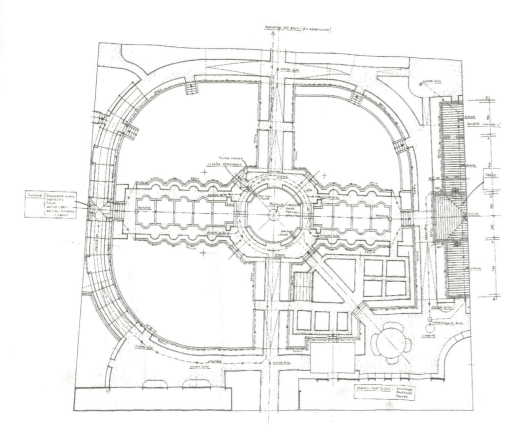

In respect of this magical place surrounded by old walls, a classic design of space games. Stairs and low brick walls are built around a natural swimming pool; the vegetation judiciously chosen by the owner has pleasantly softened its severity.

Winter delights

"Five years later,
our garden is more beautiful
and more varied than we had hoped for
when we imagined it together,
Michel and ourselves.
Each of the four seasons enchants us,
especially this wonderful spring
of containment,
each day different!
Thank you, dear Michel,
for your wonderful creativity!"

A slight undulation of the lawns' relief, the flowerbeds and shrubs provide a chromatic play of colour in all seasons in this clearing in the middle of the woods where life is good.

Concentric waves
Woluwé

"What can I say about my garden?
It is the extension of my living room
and there's no point in describing it.
I live in it and that's how I wanted it.
Thank you for understanding this at our first meeting and
translating it into a project that I enjoy from the moment
I wake up. In summer and winter my garden keeps
and lives its personality. If I had to sum up my feelings in
one word: HAPPY. This is, Michel, in a few words,
the expression of my feelings towards
the garden you have created."

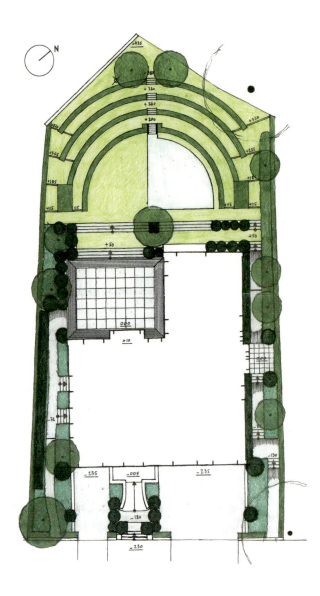

An amphitheatre has been built in place of an impressive embankment with a succession of boxwood hedges: the back of which maple trees, rose bushes and flowers can be discovered through discreet paths to the upper terrace overlooking the water staircase.

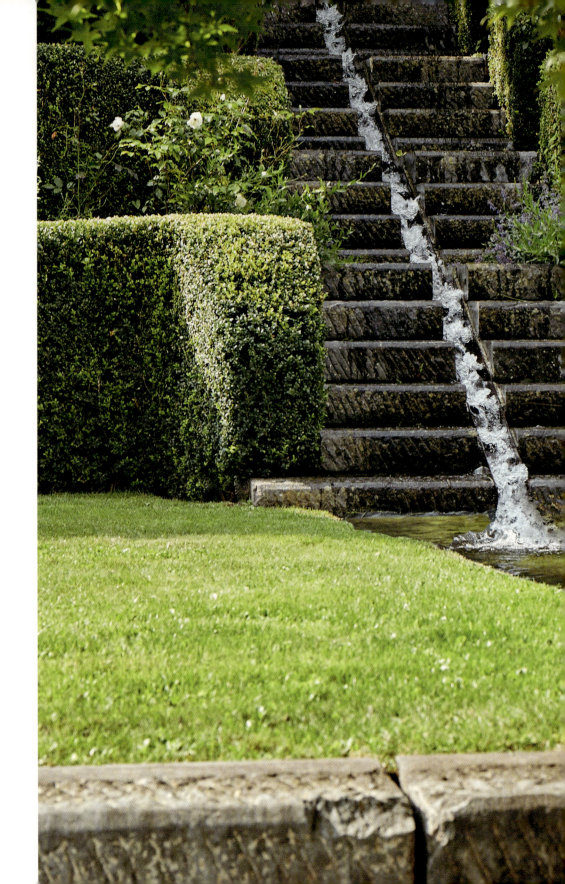

History of water
Bousval

The post-industrial site of a former forge, its reach parallel to the river Dyle, its springs and a pond necessary for its operation, an ungrateful schistose soil. The owners of the site, attentive to the beautiful landscape, wanted to create a landscape full of character.
The main theme is water.
The alternating mix of perennials and evergreen topiaries decorates the area around the house. In the foreground, the infinite view of the pond, extended by dolomite paths, a sinuous wooden footbridge and a transparent bridge invite you to stroll between the river and the ponds, the river covered with the bubbling of a waterfall and a multitude of water birds, a strong contrast between the lawns and the atmosphere of the natural reserve.

A grandiose succession of concentric curves of hedges masks technically necessary land supports.
The majesty of two majestic lines of hornbeam trees, trained as blocks.

An oasis in Sologne
France

"Creating a landscape and reviving an old farm
in a very austere region with poor and arid soil,
in a harsh winter and summer climate.
It is the result of a great challenge.
Its long life and maintenance require
perseverance and passion!
Michel Delvosalle has successfully met this challenge.
The creative landscape borders the garden well
and the rest of the surrounding nature rich of
forests and ponds. It gives a dynamic modernity
to the farm, a nice compromise!"

The matching of interior and exterior functions has been the guiding principle of this project. The central element is the position of the dining room terrace in the shade of the plane trees.
The pathways join the pool area and the lounge, which are intimate by a mix of evergreen, deciduous and flowering vegetation... where one feels good, in the foreground of the immense view of the Sologne ponds.

The art of the curve
Uccle

"Michel has accompanied us
during this long adventure
to arrive at this garden in which
we are so happy today.
We trusted him,
with his first drawing
being made before our eyes
with his partners from Jardin Plus
who are used to working with him.
What a team! They have created a garden
even more beautiful than Michel's drawings.
And that's just the beginning,
season after season it matures,
and the ducks, herons, geese, bees and foxes
come to share this beautiful place with us."

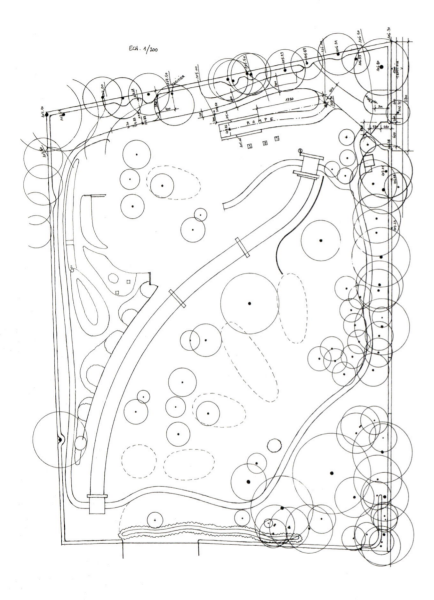

The grand gesture of laying out a hundred and thirty metre long canal interspersed with small waterfalls, indispensable elements linked to the constraint of the relief, in an orchard atmosphere.
The terraces set in flower beds, a peripheral walkway - a simple logic where everything finds its place.

A green setting
Rhode-Saint-Genèse

"Michel has transformed this garden into a real little paradise
with poetic, mysterious and exotic accents.
A real haven of peace where the flora and fauna
have taken possession of every corner
Thank you for this marvel!"

A garden from this year's spring. The planting of mature plane trees shades the terrace, a play of mirrors catches the eye, the transparency of the bridge plays with the mass of the slate steps.
The choice of plants is the final element in the atmosphere created.

Along a marine river
Brittany

"How to transform an old convent swept by
the Breton winds and rains,
bathed by the ebb and flow of the river,
into a haven of light,
plenitude and serenity?
Here the agapanthus are on a par with the clouds
thanks to their height. Roses and asters mix
their multiple tones in a succession of tiers
that overlap from the foreshore to the edge of the woods.
Here and there, clumps of daisies rub shoulders with palm trees
on their terraces, intended to offer shade
and coolness to the guest for a day, a week or a season,
to the appointment of this plenitude so often forgotten."

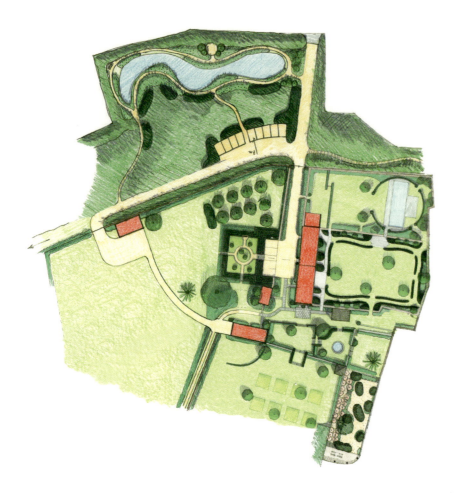

The car had taken on a prominent role. Major structural work was carried out to open up the space where shrubs and flowers have been restored to their original colour scheme, revived by the special Breton light.
The restoration of a marshy area into a tropical pond was a challenge that the mild climate favoured, in the shelter of the oceanic winds.
An infinite number of paths run along the marine river and criss-cross the countryside, alternating between undergrowth and fields.

Complicity
Waterloo

"Totally seduced by the brilliant pencil stroke and the beautiful perspectives of Michel Delvosalle, our meeting was rich in exchanges and sometimes heated debates. On both sides, we were overflowing with ideas, some of which seemed clear and obvious, others contradictory and utopian, but why not let ourselves be carried away and dream...

The reality on the ground was complex: significant differences in level of what used to be an old farmyard made of cobblestones, walls in the middle of nowhere, with the beautiful park on the edge, redesigned in English style in the 19th century.

It was therefore necessary to redefine an entrance driveway, to restore the old terraced vegetable gardens and recreate a link with the surrounding landscape. These confrontations of ideas and the constraints of the site transformed into an opportunity which helped to shape a poetic garden that reflects each personality and which seems to have been there forever."

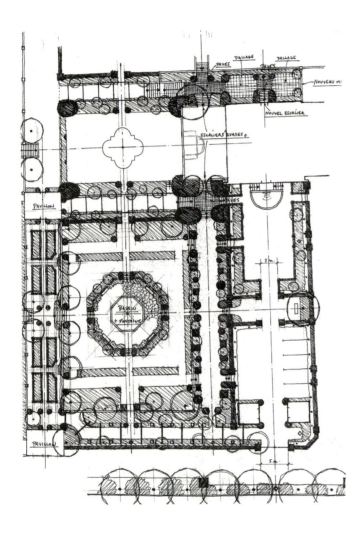

Large masonry walls ran parallel to the contour lines in a rural clearing site in the Forêt de Soignes, what potential! I had the idea to create platforms connected by pathways and staircases, as many promontories on potential openings offering views over the valley.

All the follies, the diversity of the materials found and the infinite collection of varieties chosen and planted by the owners, who are passionate about gardens …
what a great experience!

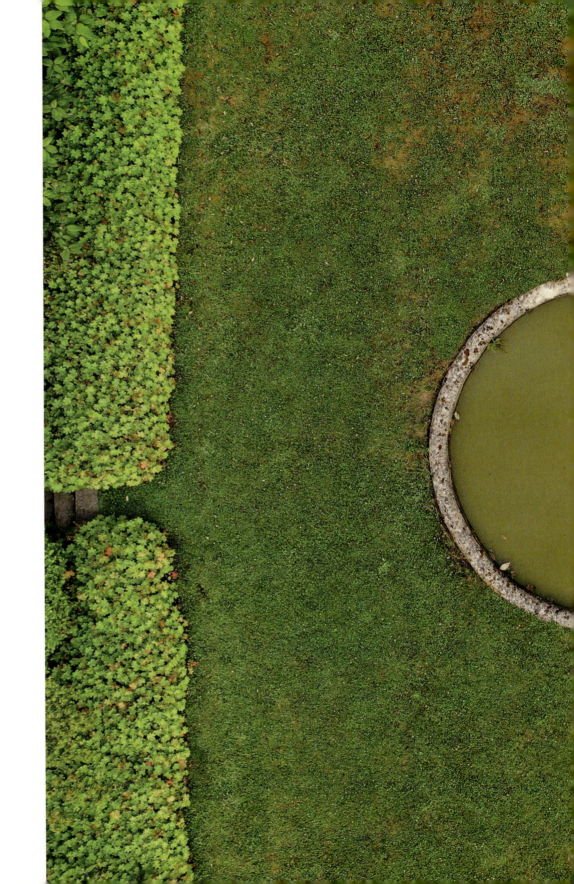

Monumental Contrast
Lasne

"When the garden was finished, it seemed to us that it had always been there."

A steeply sloping plot of land, disfigured by the work necessary for the demolition of the existing house and the construction of the new one.
A cyclopean wall made of stone blocks, the interstices of which are colonised by moss and ferns, is set up to support an imposing slope covered with heather.
A monumental entrance staircase, made of shale fragments weighing more than three tons, a sand terrace embellished with two multi-trunk beech trees, sentinels dominating a wetland, a stream undulating in the undergrowth... a very young and contrasting garden of this spring.

Return to the imagination of childhood
Tourneppe

"A hot air balloon above a sea of trees,
a footbridge plunging into a clearing,
a nest surrounded by flowers
and visited by deer, a small hidden paradise:
when the gate opens another reality appears...
It is happiness in every season,
a deep breath is taken."

A second family home in a natural area on the southern outskirts of Brussels.
It consists of two parts, one horizontal, formerly cultivated,
the other very steeply sloping.
A glass footbridge with bluish reflections overhangs it,
like a flight over the canopy of the Halle woods.
The transplantation of old apple trees in a large undulation organizes
the space with a succession of swarms of grasses and dominant
perennial plants, non-invasive, with grassy paths.

991

Infinitudes
Ixelles

"Our garden is an old city garden. We wanted to invest its very particular volumes of balance between vegetation and mineral, simple and harmonious structures and multiple unexpected points of view created by several large mirrors judiciously placed. The result is an atmosphere conducive to contemplation."

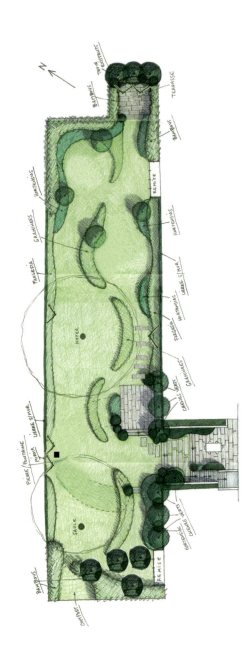

A T-shaped garden plan. Only the smallest part was visible from the house. The challenge was to try to direct the eye to the non-visible parts of the garden through the use of mirrors set at 45 degrees to allow the mind to wander infinitely through the walls of this city garden.

A landscape utopia
France

"Living at Fanet, a paradise created by Michel, means...
To marvel daily at the strength and truth of nature;
to follow with dazzlement the traces of the light which
spreads out transfiguring the landscape with a
thousand green tones; to seek out and admire
the changing and sonorous reflections
and sound of water in all its states;
feel the mineral and mysterious presence
of the stones, to enjoy being outside all the time,
so as not to miss a second of this unique
and beneficial sensation of living in a landscape
that makes us feel fully connected to nature
and ourselves; a landscape that feels
so good and rejoices, like all paradises,
when we share it".

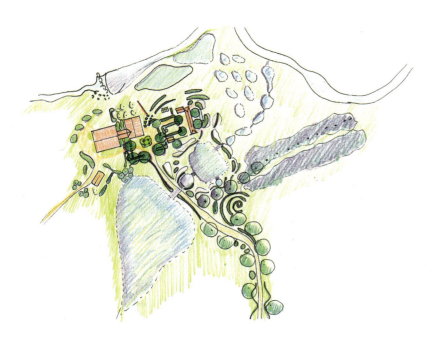

From a sheep meadow landscape, the garden has insidiously taken hold over 20 years.
It all began with the management of drainage and run-off water to a pond cascading over steps.
The access road is crossed by a ford, flowing naturally into a multitude of small ponds flowing into the river.
Plane trees and a multitude of low hedges planted in undulations around the buildings. An abundance of flowers, planted in the centre of a cereal farm.

Ephemeral reflections
Ixelles

"A carpet of pebbles inspired by Sonia Delaunay, accompanied by two large mirrors have brought to life this small city garden."

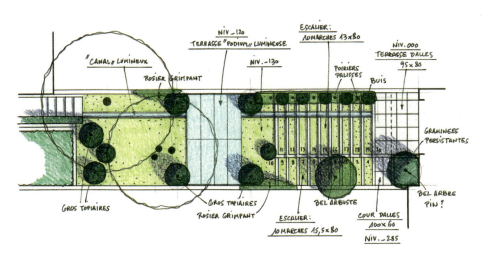

A *pied-à-terre* garden in the city must be easy to maintain,
a "basin" made of bluish glass, two large mirrors face each other, reflecting
the topiaries in infinite distortions according to the temperature.
A carpet of pebbles has replaced the mirror on the ground.

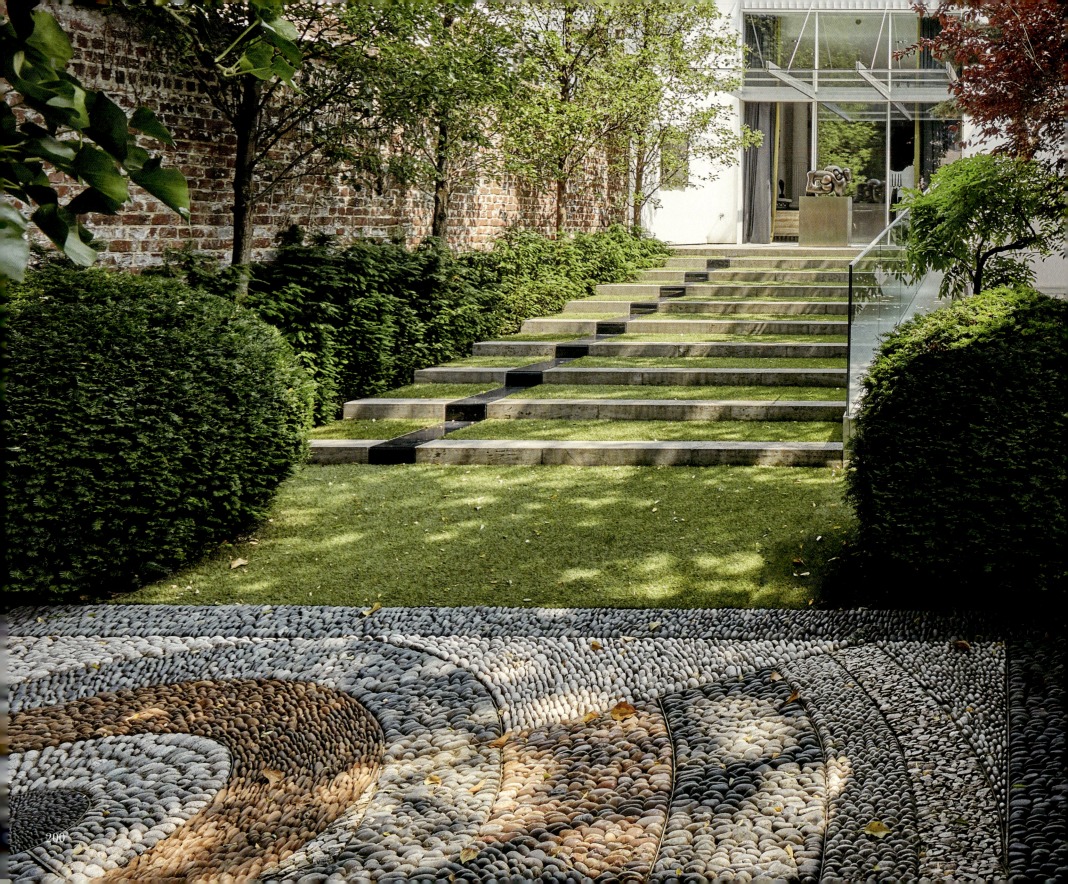

Harmony
Rhode-Saint-Genèse

"Dear Michel,
Our beautiful garden was created by you in successive stages.
We often saw you coming and going in and around the house.
You were part of the family, so to speak.
In bringing it to life, you managed, with a rare kindness and talent,
to give a soul to this place that has become so dear to us.
Now, in spring, we have an avenue of trellised pear trees and a shower
of white petals that fill the air with intoxicating perfumes.
A little further to the side we see a domed structure covered with wisteria,
which acts as a blue-toned setting for a white marble Buddha. In the summer,
a rose garden becomes a kaleidoscope of sublime colours; beds of wild flowers
with foraging insects enchant the viewer and … in autumn, a small orchard
with generous fruit trees revives our childhood memories.
Finally, the glittering reflections of winter frost on a small forest of reeds
at the bottom of the garden promise us the return of fine weather.
What a beautiful harmony reigns since your passage.
Thank you Michel, we will always be grateful to you."

The time of the fundamental reorganisation for car traffic is long gone, and everything has returned to its rightful place with ease.
A path planted with pear trees invites you to discover the restored greenhouse, its swirling chimney and the Buddha buried under the wisteria. Outdoor furniture simply placed on the lawn overlooks a multitude of gauras in infinite bloom, an invitation to stroll.

Infinity of plants
Woluwé

"Yesterday a field of wild grass,
today a green setting
in the middle of the city
where your dreams escape
in perspectives lined with
delicate hornbeams,
Portuguese laurels from another age,
or other rare acer,
carpeted with azaleas,
The birds have understood this:
each day more numerous,
they make their refuge there."

A new house, built in a backyard where one felt assaulted by the prying eyes of neighbouring windows.
A large and diverse green wall has been planted.
Small paths run through it, ideal for small children.

The planting starts at the front of the building to enlarge the garden area. The terraces are surrounded by vegetation, a subtle alternation of evergreen plants, maples and long, delicate flowers.

Water games in the Ardennes

"The closed gate says: Go on your way,
this is our garden...
The lane without hurrying,
climbs from pavement to pavement,
from trunk to bush,
to the house.

Here everything yawns and wakes up
at the first laugh of the sun.
Pale procession
of snowdrops,
Daffodils, hellebores, violets,
and a cloud of daisies
jostle the ferns.
They are the first to rise in the still prickly
cold, their spring.

In summer, in the small pool, the stone
spitter sings in his bath.
The perfume of the red roses is heavy,
that speaks of time too short and of love.
The swamp oak, rustling with birds
sighs with ease with its feet in the water.
The spring runs down the meadows,
slows down, becomes languid, then from step
to step, joins the pool of the patriarchal carps.
The red boat smells of hot tar
and rotten wood, the children's holidays,
their laughter and their cries.

September brings autumn,
its grape and apple harvests,
its mornings of mist so dense and
so wet that one can quench one's thirst.
Hedges and bushes give up their last fruits to
the thrushes powdered with frost.
The sun, that old fool, still dances and tries to
warm the bark of the trees without strength.

Then comes winter and silence.
The flowerbeds fade helplessly
to the frosts and thaws, rains and snows
which make their merry-go-round go round.
A mute remnant of life drags itself in black and
white the woods and discolours the fields.
December is silent, stunned,
makes the chimneys hum.

The garden, as in every season puts
its arms around the house.

This paradise of a thousand facets
it was you who brought it out of oblivion.
This place of life, this fountain of youth,
the fruit of listening, creativity
and competence, is the child of an
artist gardener who loves his job.

Thank you Michel."

The restoration of a pond began with a fundamental technical restructuring: re-waterproofing, tapping a spring, feeding the pond continuously to the house by means of the slope and the overflow feeding a series of small waterfalls, a sinuous flow bringing the water to the circular small waterfalls leading to the circular pond at the foot of the terrace.

The joy of living

"If I acquired this property,
it is largely thanks to the magnificent park that surrounded it!
There were some splendid trees that were more than two
hundred years old, but above all
an enormous two-hectare lake.
It was a perilous task to try to make any changes to it.
As we wanted to enjoy the landscape to the full,
Michel succeeded in creating a huge terrace overlooking
the pond.
The terrace is lined with paths at two different levels, allowing
you to go down and get closer to the water through the flowers.
The whole gives an elegance and perfect harmony with the
existing park!"

In this magnificent park designed by the landscape architect Louis Fuchs in the late 19th century, the idea was to discreetly create a terrace on the ground floor, easily accessible on the ground floor.
Made of natural stone, bordered by a taxus hedge, topiary plants and large clumps of hydrangea Annabelle accompanying the staircases in rough single-block stone, leaving an impression of antiquity.
The sketch above represents a utopian view of the tennis court area.

The moat

"In the 14th century, a small estate
was born in Flanders, with its lands and farms.
From monks to gentlemen, from owners to tenants,
from transformations to refurbishments, from fires to reconstructions,
it has lived through the centuries and experienced many lives,
from the wisest to the craziest.
Made imperishable by those who have fallen in love with the place,
the house, with its air of a stern old lady, is humanised by its historical roots
and a legend that it is the Malpertuus of Reynaert de Vos' novel.
The main house is surrounded by a moat that whispers in sneaking
under the bridge.
The park quietly traces its way between the venerable beech trees,
rhododendron beds, Japanese maples and magnolias.
In this modern garden, the present perpetuates the past.
Everything tells us about the passion of successive inhabitants for harmony,
architecture, history, writing, colours and words, and above all
for serenity and joy of living.
A place of peace where one is never done loving, nor being loved,
nor to learn, nor even sometimes to surprise."

After the renovation of the house,
it is a long way to find the softness of a simple park.
One forgets the hand of the landscaper.
A gently undulating lawn, bordered by Rhododendrons,
surrounded by soothing moats.
The farmyard has been planted with grasses mixed with perennials and hardy
roses, a subtle combination creating a bucolic atmosphere.

Provençal dream
France

A Provençal farmhouse, its walls and stairs made of local stone
with small refreshing fountains, in the shade of hundred-year-old plane trees.
The chain of blue Luberon mountains in the background, the magnificent
landscape of the lavender fields.
The only thing left to do was to find the connecting plant element.
The large arc of the circle shelters a thalweg that collects the torrential waters.
An essential protective element, the path is bordered by a line of rosemary.
In this enclosure, a mixture of flowers has taken its place, interspersed with
gravel paths. It is good to stroll here.

The art of living at Molière
Ixelles

"A weeping ash tree, a generous shade,
sometimes trembles in the breeze.
It is the centre of this small world punctuated
by large boxwoods,
immobile and wise satellites where
chickadees and wrens hide...
Behind them, in its round orb,
a murmuring pool...
one often sees there, almost shyly,
the silent flashes of japanese cyprins...
A little further on its carpet of grass,
a blackbird gives itself the air of a silent owner,
but does not dare to enter the winter garden
of an old-fashioned greenhouse,
almost mirror-like...
Where is reflected, happy and proud,
our discreet garden...
the paradise of the Persians..."

When crossing this townhouse, the only access to the garden, one perceives a succession of three spaces on the scale of the interior rooms. An outdoor dining area in the shade of the weeping ash tree, a space devoted to the circular pond, a lawn area and, in the background, the living greenhouse set against the wall. A haven of peace enhanced by the rustle of water emerging from a concretion of lava stones where mosses and ferns grow.

Golf des 7 fontaines
Braine-L'Alleud

"We have been working with Michel for many years and are delighted with our collaboration. He guides us in the choice of plants and helps us to discover new perspectives on the domain. In particular, Michel has created some superb views from the terrace of the club house. Michel's work on the golf course, pyramids, bridges, water features or plantings have always received an enthusiastic welcome from our members. Thank you for your advice Michel and I hope that we will continue to create beautiful landscapes together."

A one-off landscape collaboration lasting more than 30 years.

In particular, a set of monumental boxwood pyramids arranged in an arc at the start of the path opposite the entrance to the castle.

The flight
Rhode-Saint-Genèse

"Located in Rhode-Saint-Genèse, this garden deliberately follows the style of Michel Delvosalle : grasses, boxwoods, water features... The owners have taken advantage of the construction of an annex containing mainly a covered swimming pool, to develop their garden. The roof of the building has been converted by Michel into a walk in the "dunes" covered with oyats and bohemian olive trees... Superb and challenging!"

A long common journey from the development of the surroundings of a house in the middle of a meadow, in an open landscape.
The planting of a thick vegetation screen, a mixture of hornbeam, holly and yew, at the edge of the road.
And recently, the appearance of a covered swimming pool whose roof extends the lawn.
Three majestic sequoias have just been planted in the foreground.
A contrast is established between the rigor of the topiaries, the suppleness of the grasses and the elegance of the concrete as if cut with a knife.

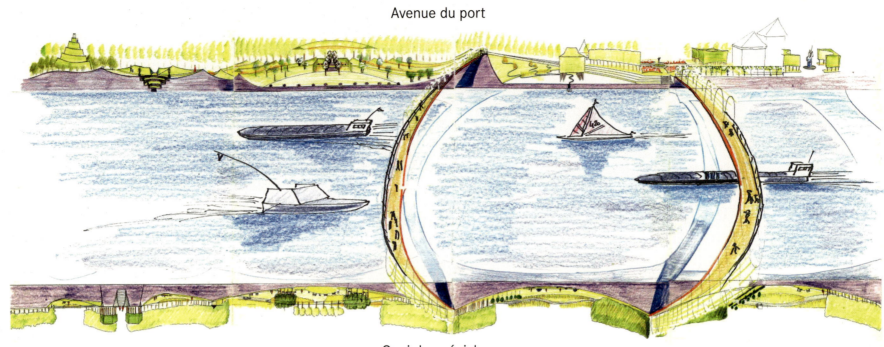

Avenue du port

Quai des péniches

Brussels, City of Water

Having been commissioned in the 1990s to study the landscaping of the canal running through Brussels, I created this utopian vision of a canal animating the city.

To the south: a beach, a lake city and its bird island. At the crossroads of the Chaussée de Mons, a tropical greenhouse. On the route, the creation of multiple themed bridges, important urban links.

A double promenade would be created: one classic at the current level, the other at water level by a descent of the banks and its promenade with shops and restaurants.

At the level of the great pavilions of the Ninove Gate, a large basin, under which an immense aquarium is developed.

The small castle would be extended by a garden on either side of the water.

To the north: a large circular basin with a swimming pool in front of Tour & Taxis
surrounded by huge arched seating areas flanked by two large curved footbridges.

A North-South aquatic junction would link the Gare du Midi to the Gare du Nord, by a "vaporeto".

The project was adapted in 2010 by adding the principle of installing sponges on all flat roofs with sphagnum moss sponges, storing and delaying the flow of water and feeding the gutters of the pavements. The water flows naturally through the catchment areas into the Senne.

Some parts of this project have been completed and why not, one day, for the benefit of the people of Brussels, the whole of it!

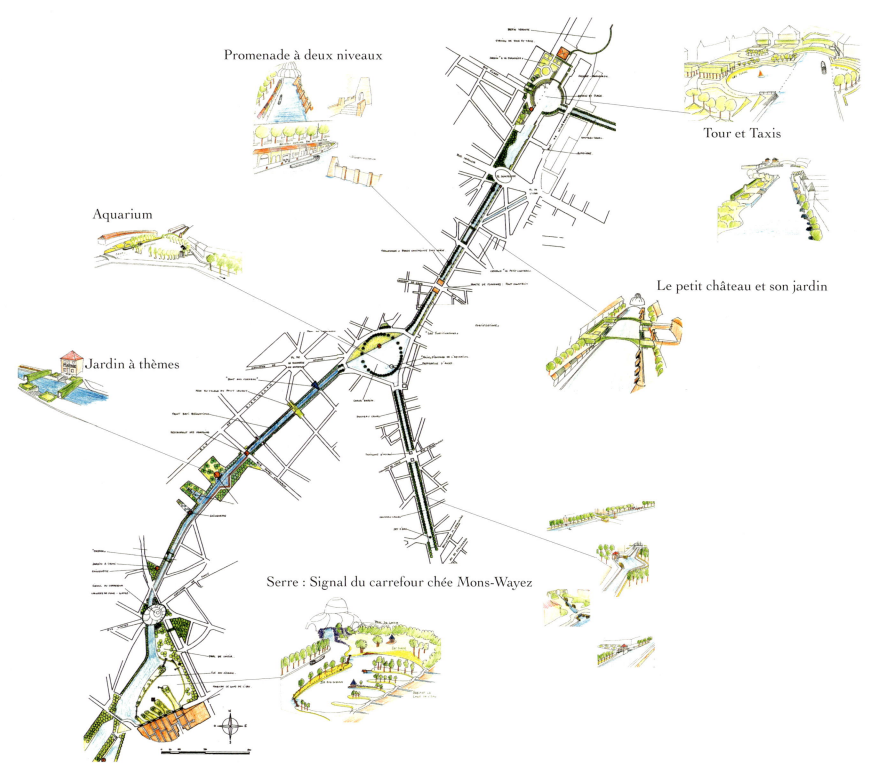

Modest intelligence and the Delvosallian flash

My first meeting with Michel Delvosalle was professional:
he was consulting me as a lawyer and professional secrecy prevents
me from saying more about the content of our exchange.
I can however mention the emotional and human context of
this first meeting.
He was stressed and rather uncomfortable. I invited him to speak and to
express himself in a freer, less reserved way and I was quickly struck by
the vivacity of his reasoning. However, he ended his speech with a:
"Oh but I'm just saying that, it's a landscaper's thought!"
In the sense that: "I'm just a gruff farmer attached to his land."
I looked at him and, even though we had known each other for only 15
minutes, asked him calmly:
- "Does it usually work?" and I kept quiet.
- "What?" he replied, a little surprised by this question, although a glint of
  mischief was already sparkling in his eyes.
- The "I'm just a landscaper!" routine.
- "But it's true, I'm a landscaper," he replied, feigning innocence and
  wondering if I had caught on so quickly.
- "Well, it doesn't work with me! Just because you're a landscaper doesn't
  mean you're not clever", I said, pointing to his brain and saying,
  "It doesn't work at full speed!"
He stammered a reply like: "Oh well, it usually works...", smiling. I repeated
that it wouldn't work with me and I knew from that moment on that we
would be real friends, that we could talk to each other and trust each other.
A dozen years later, it's still true!

As for the Delvosallian flash, I had the opportunity to see Michel discover
sites, house interiors, gardens, large spaces and I was each time struck by
the speed of his reflection.
His vision, his personal contribution, his suggestions for dealing with nature
but also with buildings are not only original but have an instantaneous
character which is quite astonishing.
A real flash that is the hallmark of a great artist!

Claude Katz

Thanks to you Michel for putting your knowledge and your gifts to
the service of nature to the point of dramatising it so well.
Thank you for being, for so many years, a close and reliable friend
who contributes to my will to stay awake.
I congratulate you for the good you do for others.

Pierre Jeanmart

Young architect,
I am looking for a reorientation.

I meet Michel ...

Our collaboration starts.

Time passes ...

Capucine joins us.

And it has been going on for 28 years.
Thank you Michel for all the good times together!

Pierre Jottrand

Acknowledgements

Special thanks to my collaborator, Pierre Jottrand.

Jo Pauwels, a talented and optimistic photographer whose precious help greatly contributed to the outcome of this book.

The Verhoeven family of printers, whose parents I met in the 1990s.

Maria and Matilde, the initiators of this project.

Thanks to my friend Claude for his insight and his always judicious remarks.
Finally, thanks to all my clients and friends and to all the people around me who generously helped me to organize my ideas.

Throughout the process of writing this book, as I came across people,
I was amazed by the abundance of fabulous ideas,
confronted in a constant good mood.
The success of this project is a reflection of the collaboration between our two linguistic communities... a very Belgian project!

ISBN:
9782875501110

Originally published in French language under ISBN 0789072124074
(Limited Edition of 300 books).

Photography and video:
Jo Pauwels
Frederic Swennen
Michel Delvosalle

Concept, graphic design and printing of the French version:
Imprimerie Jan Verhoeven in Sint-Pieters-Leeuw, Belgium.

Architecte Paysagiste - Delvosalle & Partners SRL
Avenue de la Grande Jonction, 1
B- 1420 Braine l'Alleud (BELGIUM)
+ 32 475 52 48 18
www.delvosalle.com

© Delvosalle & Partners

Printing of the English version: Graphius, Belgium.

PUBLISHER
BETA-PLUS Publishing
www.betaplus.com

© 2022, BETA-PLUS

All rights reserved.

No part of this publication may be reproduced, stored in a retrieval system, or transmitted in any form or by any means.

Printed in Belgium